Poetic Frolickings

Wandering Around the Whims of a Wannabe Writer

Luke Mayo

BookLeaf
Publishing

India | USA | UK

Made with ❤ on the BookLeaf Publishing Platform

www.bookleafpub.in

www.bookleafpub.com

Dedication

I hereby dedicate this book to all creative souls,
including mine, and their audiences, including mine. You
inspire me to do what I do as a creative writer.

Preface

Everyone has their struggles in life, and everyone deals with it in their own ways. Those of us who are naturally inclined towards creative arts, be they music or visuals or dancing or pottery, are blessed to be endowed with a natural method for sifting through the mess that the world dumps on us in regularity.

This book is the result of my prolonged sifting. You will notice that words, organised and constructed in certain and particular ways, is my chosen method for dealing with life and all it entails. If and when you read my words, you may understand some of it, and you may go completely off the rest of it, both of which is fine.

Either way, what you read has come from a place deep within me. You are welcome to take it, leave it, enjoy it or come back to it at your own leisure. That's pretty much what I do on a daily basis. Such is life.

Acknowledgements

No life that is complete and worthy can ever truly be lived in isolation. This definitely applies to me, and I owe the worthy things I do (like this book) to a number of people.

The University of Suffolk, for allowing me to be a part of their BA (Hons) course in English and their MA course in Creative and Critical Writing. Both courses enabled me to gain a foothold in the world of poetry, which led me down the path along which this book is another foothold.

The various professional organisations and charities with whom I have worked as a volunteer or office boy. They gave me the space. time, ideas and financial resources from which I was able to create so much poetry.

The many creative organisations who have tolerated my presence over the years, including without being limited to BookLeaf Publishing, the Global Panorama and Pop My Mind. I owe my creative voice and identity to you.

Lastly and mostly, my family. Without them I would be quite literally snookered (make of that word what you will), and without whom there would definitely be no

poetry.
I thank them all, for being brilliant.

1. Delcius ex Asperis

They said I couldn't do it
They said I was too weak
They laughed and jeered in my face
They wished and longed for my failure

I considered accepting it
I was tempted to resign to it
But I decided no and fought back

Giving up didn't suit me
So I proved them wrong instead

I endured their taunts
I endured my tormenting emotions
I made myself better
I found friendship

They gasped
They whimpered
They fled

They knew they'd lost their power
They failed like they hoped I would
They wanted to crush me
But they spurred me on to betterment

I am sweeter after difficulty

2. Forgive or Forget Yourself

You were a lonely boy
Ignored by all
Friends with none

Any attention they offered you
Kindness
Hatred
Curiosity
You failed to handle it
For you had not the power

You're not a boy any more
You grew and became me
I look at you through memories
I still struggle to deal with you

How strange it is
My nemesis is my own younger self
I'm haunted by your cowardice
Your ineptitude

Your string of failures

Yet you learned to deal with them
You fought
You bled
You toiled
I only became me because you strove for better
I'm the result of your striving
I'm better because you tried

So I'll forgive your mistakes
For you used them as bedrocks for improvement
I'll never forget your struggles
For your strength in struggle made you me

3. I Am Not Dreamless

I am a dreamer of dreams
Even the hard ones
Even the impossible ones
Even the failed ones

I dream of us
The life we might have had
Before you left
Before you decided no

I still dream of what could be
A bright future
A life together
It makes me happy
Even if it's just a dream

Dreams aren't bad
Dreams are ok
As long as we know reality
I'll never see you again

But in my dreams I will

In my dreams
I get to do what can't be done
I get to live the joy I can't have
It helps me live through the unfortunate truth
The fact that you're not here

That's why I refuse to be dreamless

4. Meditative Shadow

Breathe in
Breathe out
Let your muscles relax

At long last
These are the moments I live for
The chances for my body to be still and calm
The chances for my mind to wander freely

At least that's what I choose to think
I'm never totally free from the Shadow

My mind soars with ease
Rolling hills
Sweeping fields
Glorious mountains
Only when I look hard do I see it
The Shadow which has haunted me since the childhood
trauma

The thing is
The Shadow isn't as powerful as it once was
Where I used to be terrified of its presence
Now I'm just aware of it
Where my childhood memories were paralyzed by its
fearful grasp
Now I can pass over them with merely a wistful glance.

These meditative moments help
There's an emotional release
Inner peace is a hopeful possibility

No Shadow can ensnare me when I meditate

5. Turning of the Mind's Tides

The nature of my life
The things I do
The ways I feel
It's always one way or another
All or nothing
Full-on or empty and off

Some days
The tide comes in
So much to do
Long laundry lists of responsibilities
Anxieties and frustrations aplenty
Wave upon wave crashing and crushing me
Drowning with no escape

Other days
The tide is out
Life drained of purpose and meaning
Nothing to do

Nothing to feel
Just tedium and boredom
My soul left dry like a desolate wasteland

The tide of my life
Always either in or out
Never a happy medium

6. Contemplative Company

How do you avoid loneliness when you're alone?
By exploring the contents of your own mind
The one place that's never empty
Even if you think it is

Some people fear their own minds
Some people thrive in theirs
Some people make it work for them
Some people try to run away

The thing is
You can run but never escape
Only one true route exists for self-escape
That route is terminal and tragic

Far better to befriend the mind and all within it
Take charge of the cacophony of thoughts within
Assert your dominance and lead the pack

Friendship with self is friendship for life

Even friends we love dearly are riddled with flaws
So too for us
Work with the bad and embrace the good
That's how friendship goes

Apply it to your thoughts and see what happens
Get the bad thoughts in line
Show them who's boss
It can be you if you earn it

7. Plight of the Purposeless

Humans are creative in their monstrosity
Devising ingenious methods to inflict agony on each
other
Delighting in the extraction of anguished screams

One form of torture is guaranteed to debilitate me
Its potential for pain more potent than any other

Remove from my life any and all reasons to live
Surround me with souls thriving in good works
Permit me no place nor part in any of it
Cast me adrift in a meaningless existence

Purpose is my breath and blood
It maintains and sustains me
My life is one long list of worthy goals
Depriving me of them deprives me of life

There's much I can endure with a mission before me
Traumas and failures storm me but never sink me

Only one thing is my ruin
Watching the struggles and pains of my loved ones
Unable to help or save them
Being close enough to supply rescue
But forbidden from doing so

This is all I ask for
Let me do good things
Give me a chance for a life of positive deeds
This is my power and love
Please don't take it away

8. Between the Lines

In times of war and conflict
What heroes come to mind?
The ones who lead the charge up front
With courage of every kind

The face the foe directly
At risk of life and limb
They fight their case and don't hold back
Although survival's slim

Those front-line folks are heroes true
Of this there is no doubt
But there are heroes elsewhere too
Of soft but equal clout

Some heroes stick to sidelines fast
From sight they keep away
They fall beneath the public view
And this is where they stay

They have no need for public praise
To be unknown is fine
They do heroic deeds so brave
Away from the front line

Remember this from here on in
Some heroes are unseen
Look between the lines of fire
That's where the brave have been

9. Refuge in the Gaps

These moments are like gold dust
The pauses of peace
Barely noticed when you're in their embrace
Missed with wist when they slip away

Reality is a relentless ravagement
Events bombard me like waves to a boat
Anxieties clutching and dragging me to despairing
depths
Affording me no time or space to breathe or think

Sometimes the storm subsides
Chaos disperses like clouds of rain
Waves tempest not on the water's surface
I am left to drift a while

Moments like this make the journey bearable
I float freely as water laps around me
Like a soothing tonic for my entire being
Bracing me for storms to come

These moments punctuate life's ongoing madness
Without them I'd have drowned in defeat
These small spaces supply sublime solace
Empty gaps to be filled with divine nothing

I cherish the gaps for the refuge they provide
Counterbalancing chaos with dullness
Dull gaps enable us to process life's mad process
That's why the gaps are inspiring in their dullness

10. Unknown Fears Approaching

Do you know what it's like
To know you're about to die
But not know how the deed will be done?

Indistinct dangers and indistinguishable doom
This is the fate awaiting some of us
Who knows who against who knows what
For who knows why
Shady somethings playing lucky dip with victims

Unseen but for wounds left behind
Unheard but for dying screams
Unknown but for semi-stories and tepid truths
This is what we're up against
Or so we're led to believe

What cruel games our foes play
Taunting us with our own imaginations
Taunting us with enough knowledge to threaten us

Affording us no luxury of confirmation or denial

What or when or where or if
So many details hidden from our view
The only definition is the danger
Spontaneous in selection
Aggressive in application
Mysterious in motivation

Preparation is pointless
Escape is unimaginable
All we know is that something is out there

11. Fantastic Flights of Fancy

Come browse with me through my soul's adventures
Companionship enriches my whimsical fantasies

Stand with me in pride on my hard-earned pedestals
Join me in care-free games across golden medals
Partake in my communion with friends in everlasting
unity

These are the fictions through which I wander in my
head
It's better than treading the brutal paths of reality
Nothing for me there but heartbreak and darkness
Why wouldn't I escape into a world of my own making?

Like a pocket of hope in a hopeless world
Like a glimmering star in an infinite night
This is what my imagination provides for me
In a life relentless in cutting me down
My fantasies help me return to standing

The unreal can be a force for good
If it inspires goodness to be made real
My life is lived for doing the good revealed in dreams
That's why dreams will never be removed from my life
Life and dreams are forever entwined in me

12. Silent No More

The time has come
The time you dreaded
The time to conclude a period of oppressive fear
The time when repression becomes combustion
The time when the establishment shakes and breaks

A lengthy era has ticked and tocked away
You spent that era obsessed with power
We spent it being crushed by you

We were your punchbag
You were our dreaded nightmare
You used our dread to beat us into submission
Your words and actions were weaponized to attack us
Existence was a war you were winning against us

But we were no mere receivers of your violence
We watched your ways
Observed your paths
Noted your habits

You telegraphed your weakness to us
Your preoccupation with power is rooted in fear
You are scared and vulnerable just like us

But that is where the vulnerability ends
You lock fear away behind a fierce façade
We tackle it head on
In facing fear we face you

This is the overthrow of your regime
No longer do we accept our subjugation by you
We reject your violence and we reject you
We are silent no more

13. The Quiet Ones

I'm one of life's silent types
I know what's said of me
For I find myself regularly relegated
To a trope as old as time

Beware the quiet ones
Quiet is a euphemism for strange
And a mask for the sinister
It's reckoned that shallow dangers scream for attention
While quiet ones plot destruction
Several watchful eyes are kept on those like me
Lest we pose a hitherto unforeseen threat

Time for me to share a secret
There's a reason why we're so quiet
That reason is simply because we enjoy it
No secrets to hide nor dangers to plot
Just taking comfort in the silence
Why talk with nothing to say?

Silence is no axe to grind nor cross to bear
It is the conduit through which peace is found
It is a hallmark not of disturbance but enlightenment
Anybody can make a noise
Strong are they who use quietness to do good

Feel free to try it sometime
Us quiet ones will guide you
With time you might find the joy of it

14. Seaman's Code of Love

Though the seas keep us apart
Your place is safe inside my heart
Though the storm may haunt the tide
Our love brings courage to my side

For you I set my ship to sail
Our love ensures I'll never fail
Whatever troubles vex the sea
They will not keep your thoughts from me

However far I sail away
I'm always yours, come what may
Though man and beast may rule the water
My love for you they will not slaughter

The sea may hold a power great
But we won't fall beneath its weight
I make my journeys with my crew
Our love will bring me back to you

15. Lifeless on Automation

We build tech to do things for us
We entrust our lives to it
Now here's a question
What's left for us to do?

We've made tech which makes other tech
Building buildings and creating creations
So now that tech begets itself
What do we do for ourselves?

Humans clamour for a place in life
We created a system which runs itself
Did we phase ourselves out of the roles we craved?

We poured our souls into a vision of automation
An automatic reality now leaves our souls redundant

16. I'll Be Alright

It's not where you are
It's the direction you're going

That's what I tell myself
Beholding my reflection
My unimpressive body
My tummy of podge
I'm no athlete
But I'm still ok
At least I have a body
It does what's needed

As for my brain
Slow and steady
It might not get there instantly
But it gets there eventually
Subject my mind to any darkness
Be assured that it will find the light

Though the fists of life beat me down

Though the taunts of life mock me with impunity
I forge ahead through them all
Despite the tricks of endless obstacles
They stall me but never stop me

Defying odds is my specialty
Subverting odds is my talent
By flying or digging or running
I'll do it
I'll get there
I'll reach the goal

Doubt if you will
Laugh if you enjoy it
I'll enjoy proving you wrong

17. Motto of Decent People

In the name of Honour
I do well by myself and my kin
By the deeds of Decency
I will do all the good I can
To all the people I can
At all the times I can

Through the creed of Respect
I treat myself and others with kindness
In solidarity with Truth
I refuse to be someone I'm not
I recognize nature for its reality
And if I don't like what I see
I make it better

This is the code I live by
Day by day
Moment by moment
Those times when I fail
I make amends

I remember who I am
And I pledge to live it

18. An Almighty Mystery

A man of faith
A man with doubts
Both men are me
How's that possible

I say my prayers
I offer my praises
I make my petitions
Do I get confirmation of receipt?

If I try to be good but fail
If I succeed in being good but suffer for it
If I am scorned for attempting to be good
If I get tired of being good altogether
Does that make me bad?

If faith is believing the unseen and unknown
Should it be comforting or dangerous?
Is it brave to believe or brave to doubt?
The silence answering my questions is scariest of all

Some say that physicality is all there is
That unseen is unreal
But I can't see gravity
Or emotions
Or WiFi
Yet existence withstands

So does my faith
I don't see where it leads
But maybe that's the point

19. A Better Form of Zealotry

Your love for me is passionate
Let's see if that passion can be put to good use

You said you'd kill my enemies
Would you cure their iniquities?
You said you'd hurt anyone who caused me pain
Would you heal their hurtful behaviour?

You said you'd die for me
Would you live a good life with me?
You said you'd follow me anywhere
Would you travel with me everywhere?

You said you'd help me even if it crushed you
Would you let us both help each other?
You said you'd guard me while I slept
Would you join me in the world of dreams?

I love that you care for me so much
Would you care for me the right way?

20. Springtime Nemesis

I love the spring except for you
I cherish the plant life except for you
I embrace the winter's end and the summer's eve
Or at least I want to
You are the one thing hampering me

You make me sick
In body and mind
You blind my eyes
You stuff my nose
You squeeze my throat
You sap my energy

You are pollen
And you are my enemy

You and I are destined for battle
Days and years of my life
You take my health
But you claim not my soul

That is mine for keeping
Now and always

My life's roost was once yours to rule
Now I enjoy the seat of power
I surrender no more
Not to you
Not to anyone

We'll meet again for combat soon
You will try to defeat me
You will fail
My life is mine to live
Hay fever may always be present
It will never stop me

21. Field of Friendship

I walk beneath a sky of blue
I tread the grass and think of you
This field will be forever ours
This happy place where we spent hours

We laughed here in the evening breeze
We spoke at length and with great ease
I recall the earthy paths we walked
And trees at which we sat and talked

Memories of the love we shared
Joys and sorrows both well fared
These memories spark my warmly heart
Although I'm sad we had to part

You had to leave to spread your wings
You moved your life to better things
I let you go but keep you here
Inside my soul I hold you dear

This field here is our special place
I hear your voice, I see your face
I feel your presence here with me
My love for you will always be

I'll visit soon, I promise this
This field where we shared true love's kiss
Although your life has journeyed on
Our field love here is never gone

9 789363 307377